Gail,

It's a joy to share
with you in our
ministry at Asbury
Church.

Tom Short

# THIS IS LOVE

## Thomas C. Short

# THIS IS LOVE

ISBN 0-89536-320-8                    PRINTED IN U.S.A.

*This book is dedicated to
my wife, Mary,
and
our children, Donna, Curt, and Leanne,
who share with me
the laboratory of love,
our home.*

# TABLE OF CONTENTS

## INTRODUCTION

The Greeks had three words for love and they used the word which most appropriately explained the type of love to which they were referring. When they were talking about sexual love, they used the word *eros* which means physical, erotic love. On the other hand, when they were talking about fraternal love, sisterhood, or platonic love, they used the word *philia*. But when they were talking about the pure, perfect, and unselfish love of God, they used the word *agape*. We turn our attention to this strain of love (agape) in these devotions based on the thirteenth chapter of 1 Corinthians.

Agape love is love given freely and unselfishly. It is creative love poured out for the good of individual persons and for humankind. Agape love is actively desiring what is best for another. At the same time, it is love which causes us to do what is best for the most. Agape love causes us to believe that justice is love distributed.

The most perfect example of agape is seen in Jesus Christ. First, "God so loved the world that he gave his only begotten son . . ." As a result of love, God sent Jesus. There were no ulterior motives; there was no "Catch 22." There were no tricks. His coming was pure and unselfish love being unleashed on the world by the Creator of the universe.

This gift, Christ, chose to die on a cross because "greater love hath no man than this, that a man lay down his life for his friends." As a result of love, Jesus died to share the love of God with us, to reveal it to us. Again, there were no tricks. Jesus gave up his life so that you and I might be able to discover the love of God (agape) which will enable us to live more fully. Unselfishly, he died actively desiring what is best for us. This is agape!

Consequently, these devotions are not shared with you with the intention to have love mean whatever we want it to mean in the specific words given in this chapter of 1 Corinthians. This is an effort, however, to show that agape is possible and real in the flesh and blood of this life. Agape is not a gift God has reserved to be used in heaven but a gift from God to be used where we now live and move and have our being.

Since agape is given to us to share in this time and place, it strikes out against every attitude and action that would use and abuse God's children. Specifically, in the words and ideas of this passage of Scripture, agape strikes out against such attitudes as arrogance, rudeness, pride, selfishness, irritability, false prophecy, and other forms of imperfection. Likewise, this love leads to an affirmation of everything that would lighten the burden of life for God's children and cause them to live more abundantly. In the words of this passage, there is an affirmation of such attitudes and actions as humility, patience, kindness, hospitality, and courage.

Agape opens human lives to the point where persons can begin to accept the gifts of faith and hope. With agape in our life, we are more able to "bear all things . . . believe all things . . . hope all things . . . and endure all things." Since agape is perfect, it helps to lead us in a celebration of all that is right and good; and, since it is of God, it lasts forever.

Pierre Teilhard de Chardin wrote:

*Someday, after we have mastered the winds, the waves, the tides, the gravity, we shall harness for God the energies of love; and then for the second time in the history of the world man will have discovered fire.*

I share these devotional thoughts with you to help bring this discovery a little closer.

# 1.

*If I speak in the tongues of men and of angels, but have not love I am a noisy gong or a clanging cymbal.*

We depend upon the words of our mouth in daily living. With the words of our mouth we dictate letters to secretaries, share love with those in our family, whisper prayers for those who are sick and hurt, and share our thoughts concerning the events of the day. The words we speak are an important part of daily living.

To have the words of our mouth come under judgment is cause enough to reflect upon them. Under judgment, perhaps everyone is reminded of the times when their words have been like a two-edged sword which brought health and healing at one time and injury and hurt on another occasion. Sometimes our words have communicated the good news of the gospel and at other times profanity. The same lips that have whispered words of prayer to the Almighty have also shouted his name in vain. Sometimes our words are a source of encouragement to our brothers and sisters in the life, and sometimes they are a source of hurt and discouragement. Words, like lightning, have the potential of power which can help to bring energy and creativity; and, at the same time, they have the potential of destructiveness which can bring devastation and death.

All of us can recall the times when our words have been a noisy gong or a clanging cymbal because they lacked love. If love is actively desiring what is best for another, then our words are noisy gongs and clanging cymbals when they lack this active desire for another's good.

In a nationally televised interview, a well-known writer was asked what was the worst thing he had ever done in his entire life. He gave it some thought and then told the story of a time when his parents were away from home and he decided to throw a party for his good friends. They were having a great time at the party when his sister came in and broke it up. He was very, very angry with his sister. In his rage, embarrassment and humiliation, he went to his room. Later he came out of his room and started down the stairs. He met his sister ascending the stairs. He looked into her eyes and in his continuing rage he said, "I hate your ugly face." Years and years have passed since this young man met his sister on the steps and rebuked her with these words, but today he remembers these cutting words to his sister as the worst thing he ever did. The words we speak can do great good or great harm.

Some people came to see Jesus and they went away saying, "no man ever spoke like this man." (John 7:46) Surely, they were not referring to his vocabulary or sentence structure. Nor were they referring to his alliterations or oratorical style. From what we know of Jesus, he did not use long words or complicated sentences. When they went away saying no man ever spoke like this, they referred to his love. He spoke with the tongues of men and of angels because there was love in his heart for people. He actively desired what was best for every human being he met.

This same Jesus told us that it is not what we put in our mouth that makes our words bad. He claimed that what we put in our heart governs what comes out of our mouth. This causes me to review the thoughts in my heart. What are my thoughts? What are the feelings that I encourage and caress? To what part of my imagination do I give full reign? Oddly enough, this may have more to do with the words I speak than anything else.

Ultimately my prayer is this:
whatever is true,

whatever is honorable,
whatever is just,
whatever is pure,
whatever is lovely,
whatever is gracious,
if there is any excellence,
if there is anything worthy of praise,
Lord, help me
to think on these things. Amen.
(Paraphrase of Philippians 4:8)

# 2.

*And if I have prophetic powers, and understand all mysteries and all knowledge, and if I have all faith, so as to remove mountains, but have not love, I am nothing.*

Yesterday I received an anonymous letter, mailed from the city where I formerly served as a pastor. Evidently it came from a former parishioner, but I cannot be sure. At any rate, it came from someone who felt he had knowledge and understood the mysteries of God and wanted to share these. The tone of the letter was judgmental. It began with the words, "You question the power of prayer?" These were scribbled over an article written by a scientist who was converted because of the power of prayer healing a woman in his presence.

Understandably, I thought about that letter several times during the day. I have been gone from that city for more than two years. Yet here is one of God's children who is so anxious to share with me his knowledge and faith that he feels compelled to send me an unsigned, judgmental note. In his fervor he could hurt me by that note, but there is almost no way I could be helped by it. Without a signature, I could not even go to the writer for counsel if I were so motivated. Our knowledge and understanding and faith are of little value if they are not clothed in love.

A phone rang in the middle of the night. The young mother placing the call explained to the listener she was preparing to take the lives of her four children and herself. She had called this particular number, a mental health "hot line," hoping to find some help or comfort from the person who answered. Because of the late hour and the seriousness in the woman's voice, the listener tried to keep her on the phone and enable her to share her trouble. In this sharing, she explained that she had decided to kill herself and her children because an evangelist on television that night had predicted that the end of the world was here or very near, and all were going to die. The evangelist communicated this information as if he understood all mysteries and had all knowledge. He left no doubt in the mind of this troubled young mother. It is a sad, sad day when our apparent hold on the knowledge and mysteries of God gets in the way of our love for our fellow human beings.

Yet, how easily it happens. The illustration above makes me look inward into my own life. Have I given the impression to my brothers and sisters that I have all knowledge and understand all mysteries and have all faith? Have I pushed people away with the force of my "hold" on such truth? Have people seen me as arrogant? Or have I been able to share with them my struggle in the faith and my being awestruck by the mysteries of God and my honest doubts in the midst of faith? In our zeal to share the good news of the gospel of Jesus Christ, it is easy to step on the people with whom we are attempting to share.

The thoughts in this poem help me to keep the power of love in clearer focus:

So much like us, warriors and lovers,
The ocean fights, then pets the sand.
Trying to conquer the slope of the shore
It beats upward, upward, toward the land.

Waves gather their forces from afar,
And come splashing, spanking the shore,
As the waves ebb, they gently stroke
And pull more sand to the ocean's floor.

What can the cold ocean offer
Deep under a blanket of blue,
To urge release of the warm, virgin sand?
It hesitates a second or two.

Then the soldiers return,
Anger quickened by the doubt.
The waves try to force
Each grain of sand to go out.

The cannoning crash has no effect
On the tranquil grains of sand.
It's the silent, quiet pull
Of the ebb that takes their hand.

Oh, what lessons to be learned
From beach and sand and sea,
I, too, lean toward caresses,
Not a force overwhelming me.

But I must remember my parable
Is also true for you.
It is not thundering sword and fire
But loving arms will bring you, too.

# 3.

If I give away all I have, and if I deliver my body to be burned, but have not love, I gain nothing.

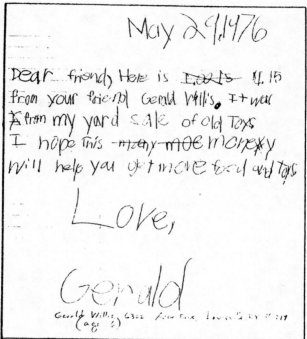

May 29, 1976

Dear friends Here is $1.15 from your friend Gerald Willis, It was from my yard sale of old Toys I hope this money will help you get more food and toys

Love,

Gerald

Gerald Willis, 6302 ____ ____, Louisville KY ____
(age 6)

Reprinted by permission from the Kentucky edition of The United Methodist Reporter.

The word that stands out to me in this note is *love*. It is written in larger letters than any other word on the page. It is much, much larger than the word money or the amount of $1.15. Can it be that Gerald understands that if he gives away all the money he has and lacks love he gains nothing?

When we share in love, we give our gifts freely to others. We do not cause the recipient to feel obligated to us. When gifts are given in love they are given "with no strings attached." Such gifts can be used as the recipients want to use them. They use the gifts in ways that bring the greatest joy, happiness, and meaning to them. Love gives the freedom which brings this joy. The more joy and happiness the recipient receives, the more joy and satisfaction the giver experiences. This is our "gain" in giving.

Fortunately, we sometimes see people who seem to be giving out of the single motive of love. Recently, on a platform in the Civic Center in Philadelphia two of these people met. They came together from different parts of the world. One was Sister Teressa who works with the poor people in India. Her work in this area is an outreach of her love for Christ and the children of God's world. The person who met her on that platform was Dom Helder Camara who works at great personal risk to help liberate the struggling people of Brazil. Again, his service to God's children strikes many as being the response of love.

When a teen-age friend of mine saw these two people meet and embrace, he wept openly and unashamedly. The power of their love for God, the children of our world, and one another was so great that he could not hold the emotion he felt. It was a beautiful moment in his life. He will cherish it for years because it is a reminder that love is the greatest motivator we have in giving ourselves and our gifts to others.

The offering Jesus Christ made of his life was one motivated by love of God and of the children of God's world. The most important thing is not that he gave up his life, but that he gave up his life because he loves you and me and all people.

We pray for this love in our lives. The important thing is not that we give ourselves and our gifts in the service of God and humankind, but that we give ourselves and our gifts in this service because of our love for God and humankind. These gifts bring the greatest hope to those who receive and the greatest joy to those who give.

# 4.

*Love is patient.*

What is the meaning of the word "patience"? It is a confusing word. At first glance, we might be satisfied if we translated it to waiting. We could point to the person who waits for the bus which is running late as the "patient" person. Meanwhile another traveler is seen as impatient because he rushes out to take the train when he hears that the bus is running late. We might point to the person who keeps "hands off" the child as the patient parent, and the one who is always jumping in to fix it or do it as the impatient parent. Deeper reflection upon the subject of patience may indicate that these are superficial descriptions.

A dictionary helps to open the windows of our mind and imagination with such definitions of patience as: persistent courage, calm and uncomplaining endurance, quiet perseverance. In the light of these words, I turn the phrase over again and again in my mind. I look for pictures to show me this in the flesh and blood of life.

A picture comes. The first brush strokes of this picture are in the operating room where the doctor sees the seeds of death in the stomach cavity of his patient. As the surgeon finishes, he does so with the knowledge that he cannot predict that his patient will live. After the operation, he goes to the waiting room and tells the husband of the doubtful medical prognosis. He explains that only time will tell, but that his patient will need much tender, loving care.

From that moment on this husband tries to do everything possible to lighten the burden of his wife's life. He does not know if she will ever be cured. He does not know how long she will live. These data are not the source of his patience. He does not serve his wife with any idea of reward of new health. He does not give the offering of his love with ulterior motives. He does what he can for her where he is because he loves her and wants what is best for her.

One thing more needs to be said of this picture. No one knows the hours this husband spends in the patient, loving care of his wife. It is not a subject shared with others either in a sense of bragging or of complaining. What a picture! A picture of simplicity. A picture of willingness to wait, and yet so much more than waiting. A picture of persistent courage, calm and uncomplaining endurance, and quiet perseverance because he loves this human being and desires what is best for her.

Another picture comes to my mind. In the spring of 1941, a young man named Thomas Merton spent a week on retreat in a Trappist monastery (Gethsemani) in Kentucky. He was struggling. His life and direction were unclear. He did not know whether or not God was calling him into the priesthood. For now, however, he was convinced that he had no vocation as a priest.

Thomas Merton lived in Gethsemani for a week and then returned to his teaching post at Saint Bonaventure. The struggle with vocation continued. He wrestled one day into the next hoping for some definite direction for his life. Near the end of that year, the way seemed clear. Thomas Merton would return to Gethsemani and ask to be received as a Trappist monk.

He sent a letter to the Trappists at Gethsemani asking if he could visit again but not indicating he wanted to stay. After receiving word from them that he would be welcome, he gave away all his earthly possessions except what he carried in his suitcase and went by train to the monastery. He tells us about his arrival:

> I rang the bell at the gate. It let fall a dull, unresonant note inside the empty court. My man

got in his car and went away. Nobody came. I could hear somebody moving around inside the Gatehouse. I did not ring again. Presently, the window opened, and Brother Matthew looked out between the bars, with his clear blue eyes and greying beard.

Hullo, brother, I said.

He recognized me, glanced at the suitcase and said: This time you have come to stay?

Yes, Brother, if you'll pray for me, I said.

Brother nodded, and raised his hand to close the window. That's what I've been doing, he said praying for you. [1]

Because you love another person, to pray day after day after day that this person may find the way in life's great journey: This is a picture of patience.

---

[1] Thomas Merton, *The Seven Story Mountain* (Garden City, New York, 1948 and 1970), pp. 449 - 450.

# 5.

*Love is kind.*

A young boy in our church went home one Sunday and received an emergency telephone call from a stranger who told him that his dog had been hit by a car on a nearby, crowded highway. The boy and a younger brother were home alone. Leaving his younger brother at home to tell the parents what had happened when they returned, the older brother went running to the highway intersection to find his dog lying completely still, with feet outstretched. The people who had called had stayed there to comfort the boy. Before long it appeared that the dog was just in deep shock and was not seriously hurt. He was soon sitting up licking his master's hand.

The young couple, who had stopped to pick up the dog from the highway, found the name and number on the dog tag and called the young boy were not the people who had hit the dog. The car that had hit the dog did not stop. This young couple saw it happen and took the injured dog from the highway so that oncoming cars would not hit him and hurt him more. In this act of kindness, they obviously saved the dog's life. The boy will never forget their kindness. Love is kind.

Kindness is love's "daily beat." Every day does not bring us crises and opportunities to do unusual services for others. Death does not come to our neighborhood every day and give us the opportunity to go with special kindness and minister to the grief-stricken. Sickness does not come every day with an invitation for us to share our kindness with those who hurt in mind or body. These crises come, but they come at distant intervals. Yet every single day of the year brings the chance for us to be kind to someone. All of the people we come into contact with on the busy streets, in the home, in the office, in the elevator, in the car pool, on the train, or in the meeting room need kindness.

Many of us are more than willing to rise to the occasion of kindness when there is a crisis. We go! It is on the "daily beat" of life, in the routine of it all that we sometimes grow insensitive and fail to do the little things to help people have a better day. Kindness is the call to make smiles a priority over frowns, courtesy a priority over curtness and caring concern a priority over preoccupation. Kindness is love's daily beat.

Michael Quoist writes about the ministry of kindness when he tells about a storekeeper and a customer. All of us have had experiences with merchants. On one occasion, we have gone to make a purchase only to be met with a growl. This merchant obviously does not want to be where he is and does not want to do what he is doing. With this kind of merchant, shopping becomes a drag and a bore.

On another occasion we meet another merchant who comes to us with all possible charm. He is wearing a false smile, and he bubbles and bubbles until we boil. He is well trained in the art of "kindness" and produces it in order to make a sale.

Gratefully, many of us have had experiences with another merchant who is genuinely kind. For those few moments of the day we have held center stage in that merchant's life, and he has done everything possible to help us make the choices that will be fitting and meaningful to us. He comes to us to help meet our needs as persons. He is more than willing to let us go without a purchase, and should we return on the morrow, he would come again and greet us in the same manner and wait upon us with the same kindness. Somehow, this merchant adds life to our life. Love always does this. Love is an active desire to do what is best for another person. Love is kind.

Today someone needs our kindness. Maybe that person is a child who wants to feel the gentle touch of affection. Maybe, a traveler who searches the faces of strangers for the encouragement of a smile. Maybe, it is a fellow worker who needs someone to listen, hear, and understand. Maybe, a friend in a distant place who needs our response to his latest letter. Yes, kindness is love's daily beat. The opportunities are as close as life itself.

Lord, help me to be kind. Give me eyes to see and love to help meet the everyday needs of my fellow human beings.

# 6.

*Love is not jealous.*

Jealousy is one of the beasts that tears apart the garment of life. Many, many people fall prey to this beast. The beast strikes where we work and creates a disturbance because another got the promotion instead of us. The beast strikes where we play because another wins a place in the starting lineup over us. The beast strikes in our family because another human being admires and compliments our spouse. The beast strikes where we study because another surpasses us in academic grades. The beast of jealousy stalks us wherever we walk. Therefore, the reminder that love is not jealous is relevant and personal to all.

Jealousy is the opposite of love; it does not desire the best for another. Where love calls us to build up another person, jealousy calls us to tear down another person. Where love invites us to weep when one weeps and rejoice when one rejoices, jealousy tempts us to rejoice when one weeps and weep when one rejoices. Jealousy threatens to undo not only love, but life itself. How do we control this beast that would undo our love and our lives?

Love does not want just what is best for others; love also recognizes and wants what is best for us. Perhaps this is the beginning of controlling jealousy. If we love ourselves, we take the time to get in touch with the good gifts that are ours and to thank God for them. There is always a chance that we will take ourselves for granted. We gloss over our good gifts. We consider our talents to be common, usual, ordinary.

John Steinbeck, who won both the Nobel Prize for Literature and the Pulitzer Prize, states the case even more strongly. This perceptive observer of life once wrote a friend, Ed, who was having a difficult time developing self-esteem. With the continuous support and reassurance of his friends, however, he finally came to appreciate himself.

Steinbeck wrote:

> *It gave him a great advantage. Most people do not like themselves at all. They distrust themselves, put on masks and pomposities. They quarrel and boast and pretend and are jealous because they do not like themselves. But mostly they do not even know themselves well enough to form a true liking, and, since we automatically fear and dislike strangers, we fear and dislike our stranger-selves. Once Ed was able to like himself, he was released from the secret prison of self-contempt. I wish we could all be so. If we could like ourselves even a little, maybe our cruelties and angers might melt away. Maybe we would not have to hurt one another just to keep our ego-chins above water.*[2]

Yes, a part of loving others is loving ourselves. As our love for ourselves grows and develops, we are more at peace with ourselves and more at peace with others. As we discover our abilities, talents, and gifts, we find that we are unique persons in our own right. This leads to a greater and more affirmative celebration of the life in us and in others. This affirmation helps to destroy the beast called jealousy.

A neighbor was driving children in a car pool from choir practice to their homes. It was winter and there had been an ice storm. The trees were still heavy laden with the ice, and although much damage and destruction had come because of the storm, the sun was

---

[2]   John Steinbeck, *The Log From the Sea of Cartez* (New New York, 1971), p. LXIII.

now shining on the ice covered limbs of trees, making the world a winter wonderland. Everywhere you looked there was sparkling, glistening ice. The driver of the car remarked about the beauty of the trees and one little girl who was seated in the back raised up and said, "Oh yes, mommy told me that God had put jewelry on the trees and the grass."

When the mother had told the child that story, she probably thought it was routine, ordinary. It was not routine or ordinary. It was a beautiful gift. Only that mother in that time and place could describe the world to her child in such a way that the world of nature came to life in the mind of the child. That's a gift! That's uniqueness!

A part of loving others is loving ourselves. As our love for ourself grows and develops, we are more at peace with ourselves and more at peace with others. As we discover our abilities, talents, and gifts, we find that we are unique persons in our own right. This leads to a greater and more affirmative celebration of the life in us and in others. This affirmation helps to destroy the beast called jealousy.

# 7.

*Love is not arrogant.*

In his book, *Out of Solitude*, Henri Nouwen tells of meeting an old professor. Looking back over his long life as a teacher, he told Dr. Nouwen, "I have always been complaining that my work was constantly interrupted, until I slowly discovered that my interruptions were my work."[3]

The intercom buzzer sounds in my office, and I answer it. The secretary at the other end of the line announces that a person is in the office to see me. I know the person because he often stops by to chat with me. This is one of the ways he has of killing time. A glance at my schedule reminds me that I am behind in my work. Already there is more work facing me than I can possibly do in this day. What shall I tell the secretary? Shall I see the person or send him away? In moments like this, I hope I can remember that my interruptions are my work.

Love is not arrogant. Love does not set oneself above other people. Love does not see any work as more important than a person who needs love. Love is open to interruption. Love is receptive to familiar and unfamiliar persons alike. Love is hospitable. Love humbly believes that our interruptions are our work.

I was not a good math student and remember little of what others tried to share with me on the subject, but I do remember about a common denominator. This is the number into which two or more other numbers will divide evenly. Love causes us to see the common denominators in our lives as we open them to the lives of others. Love helps us to remember the times when

[3] Henri J.M. Nouwen, *Out of Solitude* (Indiana, 1974), p. 56.

we have needed to talk to someone, or the occasions when we have had to kill time, or the times when we have been afraid, or the times when we have been anxious, or the times when we have been lonely, or the times when we have stared blankly into the open spaces of indecision. Regardless of our state or status at the present time, love helps us to remember our humanity and what it is like to be human. As our memory is nudged, love calls us to open ourselves to others and to allow them to enter our lives and know that we feel at times as they feel. So love is the open door not only to our offices where others can come and sit with us, but also into our hearts where they can come and see in us the same fears, anxieties, and loneliness that plague all humankind. Love causes our lives to be transparent where hurt people can find help and encouragement as we share together what it means to be human. In this openness to one another, there is new strength, healing, and hope.

I have seen this love in action in Alcoholics Anonymous. My involvement in this organization began gradually as I worked with a friend who was an alcoholic. I had never been to a meeting, but I had read some of the literature and understood some of the procedures. My invitation to be a guest at a regional A.A. meeting was an honor. This was a banquet which was held in a restaurant and everything was beautiful. We dined in candlelight and there was steady conversation around the table.

After dinner there was a program. When the first person stood to speak he began by saying: "My name is Sam, and I am an alcoholic." With that honest confession hot tears came flooding into my eyes and chills ran down my spine. I had never experienced such humility, such openness. I don't think I ever quite got over the way the A.A. members introduced themselves.

The attitude I experienced that night was not arrogance. It was a humble love. It was love that opened lives to one another. It was a love that shared a common denominator. In this openness and humility, men and woman were given hope, encouragement, and healing. This is the ministry of love.

# 8.

*Love is not rude.*

If you went downtown to shop, walked backwards just because you liked to walk that way, and you bumped into a crocodile, what would you say? The proper response, of course, is "Excuse me."

A ridiculous situation? Naturally it is, but the point was well made in a book for young people on the subject of manners. Almost everyone can recall from their earliest memories a mother, grandmother, or aunt prodding: "What do you say, dear?" Usually the proper response was "thank you" or "please." The books written about what to do and what to say in given situations are just expansions of that person trying to teach good manners. Being rude is unacceptable. We are expected to know when to remove gloves in offering a handshake and when to respond in black ink on plain white stationery.

Actually, learning the rules of the child's books is the easy part. Amy Vanderbilt and Emily Post can guide us as adults in the situations regarding social graces, but that does not preempt the possibility of being rude to another person. Love requires more than reading books of etiquette. Love encourages us to go deeper and to be more sensitive to the feelings of others. Only this deeper sensitivity will enable us to avoid being abrasive, rude.

Recently, a secular organization offered an unusual opportunity for Christian living. Students who were planning to attend college and who needed help could apply to this organization for that help. Students who received help were given whatever "missing link" was needed to complete their education. Some of these students had financial needs, some had needs in other areas, and in some cases needs fluctuated and changed. Regardless of the situation or the changes, this group tried to provide the "missing link." They asked for no legal commitment from the student receiving help, but they did ask a moral commitment. Each student receiving help was asked to provide the "missing link" for another person when he was able. This was not structured in any way. Those receiving help were to be sensitive to the needs of others and somewhere in the journey of life find another person who needed help and provide the "missing link" for that person. To accept help from this organization and not be sensitive to the needs of others to whom they could pass along help would be rude.

Love is not rude. Love in this situation is the person on the west coast providing transportation to and from college in the northeast for a full scholarship student from a poor family. Love is the person who for three years committed himself to daily bathe, dress, and put a student into a wheel chair for the day's classes and then reverse the procedure every evening. Love is being sensitive to the love shared to meet your needs and sharing that love to help meet the needs of others. Love does not default. Love is not rude.

When we read the story of the ten lepers who were healed by Jesus we may wonder about the nine who were so rude that they did not even return to give thanks to their healer. Surely, if we were healed of terminal cancer, we would offer our prayers to God. We would not receive the gift of healing without remembering our manners. We have been trained since the time of "What do you say, dear?" to respond in a proper way to the giver of gifts. If this is one hundred percent true we can still be rude and unloving if we utter the words of thanksgiving and do nothing more. We have been given life and the opportunity to share life. Saying prayers of thanksgiving is not enough. Love encourages us to be sensitive to gifts we have received and to ways we can share our gifts to help provide the "missing link" in the lives of others.

Love is more than manners. Love is more than etiquette. Love is more than social courtesies. Love is being brought together with God through Jesus Christ in such ways as to be deeply sensitive to the personalities of others and of ways we can help to meet their needs without in any way offending them.

# 9.

*Love does not insist on its own way.*

In some translations this sentence has been shortened to read, "Love is not selfish." The translation matters little; the thought comes to judge each of us. How often we have felt the tinge of guilt because that which we call love insists on its own way. In psychological circles this is called manipulation. We control others to be what we want them to be and do what we want them to do. This is just an outward and visible sign of insisting on our own way in the name of love. This is not love.

Often we conclude that we are like this because we love ourselves too much. Therefore, less self-love would make us less manipulative and less insistent upon having our own way. Isn't there another possibility? Indeed, just the opposite is a possibility. We insist on our own way not because we love ourselves too much but because we love ourselves too little. Isn't this the timber out of which we build selfishness? We love ourselves too little.

In the lack of love for ourselves we are uncomfortable with ourselves and crave more our own way. Somehow getting our own way, manipulating others, gives us satisfaction because it helps to fill the void created by our lack of self-love. Consequently, getting our way is interpreted as meaning, purpose, strength, and power, all of which should come to us through our own self-love rather than our manipulation of others. The drowning man struggles for air for his lungs not because he has too much but because he has too little. Likewise, persons who love themselves too little struggle more and more for their own way to fill the emptiness in their lives.

In the Scriptures, Jesus tells a story of a rich fool who was quite selfish. This farmer had a good year and he thought about what he should do with all of his grain. Finally, he concluded that he would tear down the barns he had and build bigger barns. In other words, he would selfishly store up the good product of mother earth. He already had more than he needed, but this was not enough. He wanted still more. He needed more. Why? Because he loved himself too much? Doubtful. But because he loved himself too little. He did not have inner peace. He was not sure who he was and what his life meant. He did not rest easily with the meanings and purposes which provided his motivations. Therefore, he had to have more. Thus, in frustration he reached out for more and more and more. In doing so, he is a perfect example of selfishness.

The kidnapping of Patricia Hearst has many stories surrounding it, but one which spoke most deeply to me was that of the many people who sent money to the Hearst family after the kidnapping. Over a million dollars was sent by well-wishers not because the Hearst family needed the money, but the people wanted to reach out to love and share. Checks came from all over the country, but two of them caught particular national attention. These two checks for $70.00 came from people who were on welfare.

The only thing which allows persons on welfare to give up food from the table is their own love for themselves. They are so comfortable with who they are and where they are that they are able and willing to share. All of their strength and energy is not being wasted in trying to decide whom they can manipulate and control to have more and more things coming to themselves. Only when we are able to have this kind of security in ourselves are we able to allow others to be themselves. Only then are we able to love freely and not use it as a tool to insist on our own way.

Jesus loved unselfishly. He allowed people to be themselves. He did not insist on controlling the money of the little band of followers. He did not try to stop his betrayer from going out into the night to betray him. He did not insist that his disciples come to his crucifixion. Jesus loved himself and was set free to love others with no strings attached. His is the most perfect and beautiful love. Sometimes we even catch a glimpse of this in ourselves. This happens because he lives to share this love with us in such a way that we grow in our love of self.

# 10.

*Love is not irritable or resentful.*

At the close of a counseling session a young woman rose to her feet, looked at the counselor, and said, "I didn't think there was anyone in this city who was willing to listen to me." Then she thanked him for helping her, or at least giving her the opportunity to talk. Love is hospitable. It opens the door and allows others to come, share, unload, talk. Love listens. Love is not irritable or resentful. Love allows and encourages others to approach us. People do not confide in the grouch, in the irritable. Love listens, and listeners are in great demand in our society today. Many people want to talk, but sometimes there appears to be a shortage of listeners.

Perhaps the frustration of this shortage of listeners is stated most clearly by Marjorie Holmes in her book, *I've Got to Talk to Somebody, God.* The book, which is in its fourteenth printing, begins with these words:

*I've got to talk to somebody, God.*
*I'm worried, I'm unhappy. I feel inadequate*
*so often, hopeless, defeated, afraid.*
*Or again I'm so filled with delight I want*
*to run into the streets proclaiming, "Stop,*
*world, listen! Hear this wonderful thing."*
*But nobody pauses to listen, out there or*
*here-here in the very house where I live.*
*Even those closest to me are so busy, so*
*absorbed in their own concerns. They nod*
*and murmur and make an effort to share it,*
*but they can't; I know they can't before I*
*begin.*

*There are these walls between us — husband*
*and wife, parent and child, neighbor and*

*neighbor, friend and friend. Walls of self.*
*Walls of silence. Even walls of words.*
*For even when we try to talk to each other*
*new walls begin to rise. We camouflage, we*
*hold back, we make ourselves sound better*
*than we really are. Or we are shocked and*
*hurt by what is revealed. Or we sit privately*
*in judgment, criticizing even when we pretend*
*to agree.*[4]

Imagine it! A book which begins with this lament has sold hundreds and thousands of copies. There is a need for listeners. The need is so great that a psychiatrist wrote a book about therapeutic listening. His idea is that if people knew how to listen to one another and were willing to do so, there would be far less need for psychiatrists. He wrote to the bartender, the school teacher, the store clerk, and the taxi driver about the importance of listening and how to listen. The secret is not in knowing what to say, but in allowing the other person to share.

When we listen to another person, we actually confirm his life, his being. By listening to another, we say: "You are real. You are important. What you have to say is important because it is as much a part of your life as your flesh and blood." All human beings need this kind of affirmation in their lives. All of us have a need to feel real, important, and valuable. All of us have a need to share where we are and what is happening to us. That's why good listeners are often among our favorite people. In their willingness to listen they share their love with us in such a way that our life is made clearer, more real, and more liveable.

Often the good listener allows those confiding to say far more than they had planned to say. The listener

---

4   Marjorie Holmes, *I've Got to Talk to Somebody, God,* (New York, Toronto, London, 1969), p. 3.

is like a magnet that draws from the depth of the talker things that would never have come forth if the listener had taken over and started talking. As often as the listener helps us to feel real and valuable, we open up to share more and more of our lives. Listening is applause in the lives of persons who are sharing and they respond to that applause by sharing more of themselves. If it is hurt which is being shared then they feel lighter because they got it "off their chests." If it is joy and happiness they are sharing, they feel even more joyous and happy because it has been shared with someone else and it multiplies.

All of this brings meaning, health, and depth to life. If love is an active desire for what is best for another person, then love will always listen.

Someone is coming to talk. Love listens.

# *11.*

*Love does not rejoice at the wrong.*

Dietrich Bonhoeffer was a pastor in Germany when Hitler came to power. Soon it became obvious to Bonhoeffer that Hitler and the church were incompatible. One doctrine was founded on pride and hate, and the other was founded on humility and love. They could not co-exist.

As Hitler gained more and more power, he finally came to the Protestant church and asked for support. There was heated debate, but the church decided to support this man who promised to bring new pride and security to the homeland. Bonhoeffer had to say "No." He could not live in the church which had made this decision. He and some others withdrew from the church, founded and became the core of what was known as the confessing church. This was the church which was to hold out against Hitler and his regime even as Sir Thomas More had held out against Henry VIII several hundred years before.

As it became increasingly obvious to Bonhoeffer that the only way to defeat Hitler was to kill him, a plot was formed. Yes, it was a plot to assassinate; it was a plan to murder. To those who made the plans and took the risk there seemed little choice. It hurt many of them to plan to take another man's life, but they had to do it in order to stop the suffering which Hitler was causing in the country he was leading. In this particular situation the most loving thing to do for the most people was to kill Hitler who ordered the murder of the Jews.

Christian persons may feel called upon to do things in some situations which they feel they would not do in normal situations. Many of us have been around and around the argument: Would you tell a lie to save the life of an innocent person? Many of those who don't lie and have a real conviction about telling the truth admit that they would lie in this situation. In Bonhoeffer's case, it was killing in order to give life. Obviously, he was not a killer. In fact, he was where he was in the life of his people because of his sensitivity toward those who were being killed. The brutalization of the Jews was outrageous to him. This same sensitivity caused him to become involved in the murder plot. He was killing to give life.

The same decision is made by the police officer when he pulls his gun to shoot a person who is a threat to the life and safety of an innocent person. The same decision was made by Lincoln when he decided to declare war on the brothers and sisters in the south. Situations sometimes require unusual actions. In unusual situations, we might become involved in a murder plot even though killing runs contrary to the basic philosophy which we follow in our normal, day-to-day living.

If we ever feel called upon to do what we consider to be wrong in normal situations, we do not rejoice in this wrong. Love does not rejoice in the death of Hitler, although death to him could give life to others. Love does not rejoice in the death of the criminal, although he is killed to provide life and safety for others. Love does not rejoice in war, although it is declared to preserve a nation of people.

Love does not rejoice whenever any of God's children are hurt, regardless of the situation. Love finds it impossible to rejoice in spilled blood, the blood of Christ on Calvary or the blood of Hitler in Germany. In the imperfection of this life, we may feel called upon to do what we would normally feel is wrong, but love cannot and does not rejoice in the suffering brought to any person regardless of the nobility of the cause.

# *12.*

*Love delights in the truth.* [N.E.B.]

What is "the" truth to which Paul refers? The truth is this: "God so loved the world that he gave his only Son, that whoever believes in him should not perish but have eternal life." This is the good news! This is the truth! Love delights in this truth which brings hope, strength, and freedom to our lives. A picture of this truth, this good news, is given in one of Jesus' stories.

A certain man had two sons and the younger of them asked for his share of the inheritance. He got it and spent it in riotous living. He sank deeper and deeper in the life that centered in his own selfish passions. This downward spiral hit bottom one day when this boy was out feeding the hogs. He came to himself and remembered that his father treated his servants better than he was being treated. He decided he had had enough of this life and he turned to go home to his father.

Meanwhile, his father never missed a day of hoping that his son would return home. Every day his eyes scanned the landscape looking for his boy. Every day his ears longed for the sound of the familiar voice of his son.

One day when he looked out through the open fields to the horizon he noticed an unusual spot. He was familiar with the terrain and this spot was new. He watched the spot and it grew larger and larger. Soon he was able to tell that it was a person, and before long he knew there was something familiar about the gait, the stance, the swing of the arms. Suddenly he knew! It was his son!

Spontaneously, he ran across the field to meet him. He smothered his son with kisses, put a ring on his finger, shoes on his feet, and a robe on his back. The father appeared deaf to his son's request that he return home as a servant as he shouted out the order that the fatted calf be killed and that there be a great party. This son who had been dead was now alive and all would celebrate in the good news, the gospel, the truth.

This is "the" truth, the good news that Christ shares with us. We can leave the father's home, but we cannot leave the father's heart. We can break the father's law, but we cannot break the father's love. Love delights in this truth, this good news.

Illustrations of this truth surround us. This good news becomes flesh and blood in our own time and place. Sometimes it happens in "high" places and we read about it in the newspapers. One of those involved in the Watergate burglaries feels as if he has been *Born Again*. After years and years of struggling to find life, he has found it in Jesus Christ. After spending much of his life apart from the Father, he has come home to the Father. That's good news. Love delights in this!

Sometimes this good news is seen in the "rank and file" of life among very ordinary people. In a college dormitory one woman went to talk to another. She was groping for a new way of life. She was not happy with who she was and where she was. The discussion went late into the night. There was deep sharing, weeping, laughing, praying. Before the sun rose there was a new dawn in this girl's life. A "blind" woman was given "sight." Love delights in this.

In the moving book *God Is a Verb*, Marilee Zdenek writes these words opposite the picture of a dancing woman:

I'm very good at celebrating, Lord —
Have you noticed?
My soul can fly so high above the world
    I could play in a field of clouds and
        nestle like a child in the comfort of your love.
I can laugh with delight at your miracles —

*Sing to the sunset*
*Dance till the sunrise*
*Whistle in the sunshine of your care.*

*But in other times*
*When the pendulum swings*
*And darkness is upon the face of my day,*

*Then, Lord —*
*Please come*
*And teach me how to celebrate.* [5]

A part of such a teaching may be for us to look within ourselves and around ourselves to see the good news of God becoming flesh in our time and place. Love delights in this. And we are called to celebrate!

---

[5] Marilee Zdenek, *God Is a Verb* (Texas, 1974), p. 15.

# 13.

*Love bears all things.*

I used to keep a little card on my desk. On the card was a picture of one boy carrying another boy on his back. The caption read: "He ain't heavy. He's my brother." I responded emotionally to that and found it helpful. Then I began to give it some thought. It is untrue; the boy is heavy. He is my brother, but I cannot carry him very far. He is too heavy. I can go twice as far without him as I can go with him strapped on my back. He is heavy. I carry him not because he is light but because he is my brother, because I love him and want him to have what is best in life. I love him; I bear his weight upon my body. Love bears all things.

Love helps people survive and live even when the helping hurts, and it does hurt. Why should we try to fool ourselves? A mother is dressing her child for the first day of school, and she will watch the child go out the door and into a new life. There is pain and anxiety in that separation. The love the child has for that parent helps the parent to bear the moment, and the love of that parent for the child helps the child to bear the moment. They love each other, so they are able to share the pain and anxiety of one another in such a way that each can cope. Love bears all things.

Later in life the tables are turned, and the child who went out to school years ago is standing at the bedside of the parent who is now at death's door. The parent is beginning another kind of journey, going out another door. The sick parent is confused, but from time to time there is still clarity and consciousness. At times the eyes open wide and the voice speaks or the smile flashes. The grown child is at the bedside filled with pain, anxiety, and loneliness in this coming separation. The child is at the bedside not because it is easy, but because love bears all things. The child cannot take the journey for the parent any more than the parent could have gone to school for the child, but the child is there to help the one leaving to go with added peace and assurance. The pain and anxiety of this situation are weaker than the love. Love bears all things and is present even when it hurts to be present. Love helps to bear the weight of our brother and sister even when their weight is heavy.

Of course, we are not able to produce this love within ourselves. This is grace, a gift of God. The Christian person sees this gift most clearly in the face of Jesus of Nazareth. This Jesus, who is of lowly and humble beginnings, is the person who brings to us the message of God's love. He tells us this as the love of God flows through him to bring sight to the blind and sanity to the possessed. He tells us this as he sets a young woman on a new way of life filled with hope and encouragement with the simple words: "Neither do I condemn you. Go and sin no more." He tells us this when he gathers his friends around him on their last evening together and asks them to remember him as one who shared his all, even his life for them. He tells us this when, dying upon a cross, he reassures the soldiers who kill him and the criminals who die with him that they are not beyond the reach of the love of God.

As often as we see this Christ living and dying to open the windows of our lives so that the fresh air of our Creator's love can blow through our lives, then we are affected by it. Just as force begets force, so does love beget love. Just as we come to understand what it means for God's Son to bear all things in our lives because of his love for us, we come to the startling realization that because of him and with him, we can bear all things in the lives of our brothers and sisters because of our love.

This is not the end. This is the beginning of worship, service, and life!

# 14.

*Love believes all things.*

*Two men looked out of prison bars.*
*One saw mud; the other saw stars.*

Love encourages us to look at the stars in life more than at the mud. Love, which desires the best for another person, looks at others not through the lens of suspicion, doubt, and fear, but through the lens of trust, confidence, and hope. Love believes in the presence of goodness and beauty in every human being. Love looks for these characteristics in every person, and in this process encourages the survival of goodness and beauty in human life. It gives these characteristics the opportunity to surface and grow.

Jesus met a man named Zacchaeus sitting in a sycamore tree. This tax collector was hated by the people who knew him. They could see no good in that man who was robbing them to stuff his own pockets. Jesus stopped to talk to Zacchaeus and went to have lunch with him. The people stood aghast, but Jesus believed all things about Zacchaeus. The love of Jesus looked for the goodness and beauty in the life of this tax collector, and these characteristics were there. This goodness and beauty surfaced and began to take over Zacchaeus' life.

That story is repeated over and over again in the Gospels. The love of Christ believed in the goodness and beauty in the life of his disciples, and those characteristics surfaced and began to dominate their lives. His love believed in the goodness and beauty in the life of a fallen woman of the streets and these characteristics surfaced. His love looks at a person and believes that there is goodness and beauty in that person. His love believes that God has made us in his image and his characteristics are within us, be that ever so well hidden.

In many ways this attitude of Jesus has been given to us through the musical, *Man of La Mancha*. In fact, many people see the story as an allegory of Jesus. The man of La Mancha believes in the goodness and beauty of people. He is a positive thinker. When he saw a prostitute, he called her, "My lady." Open-mouthed and wide-eyed, she stared at him in total disbelief: "Me, a lady? I was born in a ditch by a mother who left me there, naked and cold, and too hungry to cry. I never blamed her. I am sure she left hoping that I would have the good sense to die."

The man of La Mancha continues to look at her and to believe in the goodness and beauty within her. He prods her imagination with the idea: "Your name is not Aldonza. I give you a new name. You are my lady. And I give you the name Dulcinea."

Later in the play she appears on the stage after having been raped by some travelers. She is hysterical, and the man of La Mancha tries to comfort her and again affirm the goodness and beauty that he believes lived within her. She will hear none of this. In hellish hostility she screams at him, "Don't call me a lady! God, won't you look at me! I am only a kitchen slut reeking with sweat! A strumpet men use and forget! I am only Aldonza. I am nothing at all!" With this tirade she runs from the stage, but even as she leaves he calls: "My lady." After a moment of silence he looks across the stage to say again: "My lady." With no response, he calls her new name, "Dulcinea".

As the play concludes, the man of La Mancha is dying of a broken heart. A very beautiful woman comes to his bedside and when he looks up at her to ask who she is, she rises to her full stature and beauty. With the eloquence of a royal person, she replies, "My name? My name? My name is Dulcinea!"

Yes, love is the breath that blows softly upon the coals of goodness and beauty encouraging them to burst into a roaring flame. Love believes that a flower can grow through the smallest crack in a sidewalk to grace the world with its beauty. Love has the ability to believe that goodness and beauty live in every human being.

# 15.

*Love hopes all things.*

As with faith, the writer of this letter to the church at Corinth mentions hope again. In these concluding words of this great chapter of Scripture, these two words hold key positions with the word love. Somehow the three seem inseparable.

Love is the manger in which hope is born. The Christmas story in St. Luke's Gospel never grows stale. Some say it is the beauty of the English language that keeps it fresh and alive. Others say it is the height of the human spirit at Christmastime that gives the story such an emotional impact. Still others find great meaning in this story because it is the story of hope. In the giving of Christ, God tells us that he loves us. He gave us his Son. This love is the manger in which hope is born.

In this story God tells us that he is for us, and in another letter to another church Paul asks, "If God be for us, who can be against us?" (Romans 8:31) Exactly! Love is the manger in which hope is born. To receive the good news that God loves us and is for us, is to have hope born in us. To say that God loves us and, at the same time, to be hopeless is a contradiction.

If there is confusion here, perhaps it lies in what God's being "for us" means. A family gets a call that their son has just been involved in an automobile accident. They rush to the scene of the accident and find the family car completely demolished. Their son has already been taken to the hospital, and they stand there looking at the wreckage thinking that he must be dead or near dead. It seems impossible that anyone could survive this mangled mess.

They rush to the hospital and find their son with relatively minor injuries. He has a cut on his forehead and a broken left leg. They stand in the waiting room comforting one another. Several of them are heard to say, "Surely God was for him." Sometimes this kind of thinking is a pathway to darkness rather than light. Sometimes it hides God instead of revealing him.

In our human predicament, it is easy for us to think that God's being for us is the same as getting what we want. We think like this: God is for us when we want a job and get one, when we want a child and conceive one, when we need an increase in salary and get it, and when we walk away from what could have been our death scene. This kind of thinking tempts all of us.

There is something far deeper in the promise:"if God is for us, no one can be against us." The deeper promise is that regardless of the circumstances of life, God is for us, and we have hope. God is much more than the annual Santa Claus who brings us the gifts we desire. He is also the God who meets us in the pit and mire of life and in those "down and out" moments reminds us of his love and presence in such a way that through our tears of suffering and grief we understand that he is for us. Hope is born.

If, when the parents arrive at the scene of the accident, the son is lying dead on the highway, God is still for the son and for the parents and other loved ones. He is for us and "death is swallowed up in victory." (1 Corinthians 15:54) If God be for us, even death itself cannot overcome us. And the ultimate hope is born!

# 16.

*Love endures all things.*

A university chaplain was awakened in the middle of a rainy night by the ringing of the telephone. He tried to bring himself out of a deep sleep while listening to the voice of a student who was in need of help. The student explained that the chaplain did not know him, had never met him, but he needed help.

The student was asking the chaplain to meet him so they could talk. It would have been easy to put this student off. The chaplain didn't know him, it was raining, it was the middle of the night, and any legitimate buildings where they might have met were locked. The chaplain's wife was uneasy about the whole thing and cautioned him to be careful. This might be another "nut." There were so many good reasons why the university chaplain could ask the student to come by the office in the morning.

Instead of postponing the meeting, the chaplain made a commitment to go out that night to a designated place to meet the student. Love endures all things. Love goes out to help when others roll over in bed and go back to sleep. Love has the strength to endure, to keep going when others quit.

While typing these words, I can't evade a little plaque on my desk next to my typewriter. It is the picture of a tree with a lion in it. The lion looks exhausted; his legs are limply hanging down the limbs of the tree. His head is nestled in the branch and his eyes are closed. Under his picture are the words: Hang in there! All of us need these words when we are just plain tired of going on. Love hangs in there. Love endures all things.

Dag Hammarskjold said the same thing with more literary style:

*When the morning's freshness has been*
*replaced by the weariness of midday,*
*when the leg muscles quiver under the*
*strain, the climb seems endless, and*
*suddenly, nothing will go quite as*
*you wish — it is then that you must*
*not stop.* [6]

Of course, the idea is not to hang in there stoically until we lose our minds or our lives. The calling is to endure and try because love calls us and strengthens us for the task. Love offers us a high calling, and it also offers us a great source of strength. It is the combination of the two that calls us to endure.

Some people would look into the eyes of the chaplain who went out on this mission of mercy in the middle of a rainy night and ask him how he could do it. The answer is discovered in the source of the chaplain's strength. Jesus Christ, himself, met a troubled man named Nicodemus in the night. In this and other experiences in the life of Christ and his fellow human beings, the chaplain sees the love of God. In God's love he is strengthened to go on this and similar missions of mercy. The love of God is fuel for his endurance. To experience the love of God for us in the ministry of Jesus Christ is to be strengthened to share this love with all humankind.

The more work Martin Luther had to do the more time he spent in his private devotions. If he already was cramped for time, why did he spend more time devotionally? He knew the source of this strength and energy. Love not only called him to "hang in there," but the love of God also gave him that strength.

---

[6] Dag Hammarskjold, *Markings* (New York, 1964), p. 124.

# 17.

*Love never ends.*

Love does end. A husband and wife have loved one another deeply and meaningfully through the years, but recently something has happened. Their life together is flat; love is gone. Another person has had a remarkable religious experience which resulted in his loving the Lord with all his heart, mind, soul, and strength, but recently the light of that love has gone out. Whether we call it spiritual eclipse or the dark night of the soul matters little. The love is gone. Love does end.

True, love, as we dilute it in our own language, ends. Paul is not writing about love diluted. He is talking about God's love, *agape* love. This love of God never ends. God never stops wanting what is best for you and me. The light of his love for us never goes out. Paul said it clearly in the letter to the church at Rome when he wrote, "For I am sure that neither death, nor life, nor angels, nor principalities, nor things present, nor things to come, nor powers, nor height; nor depth, nor anything else in all creation, will be able to separate us from the love of God in Christ Jesus our Lord." (Romans 8:38-39) This love never ends. The love that he shares with us in the life of Jesus Christ is forever and ever.

This is the good news of the gospel: God loves you and me. This is not a love we have deserved. We have not earned it with quality points. It is not a love wrought by the works of our hands or the splendor of our personality. This love is a gift. We have not created it so we cannot destroy it. As the waves of the sea continue to wash the shoreline, so do the waves of God's love continue to wash upon the shorelines of our lives. As with the waves of the sea, you can turn your back on the beauty of God's love, but this does not destroy it. It is not stopped by our unwillingness to look on it. As with the waves of the sea, you can build barricades against God's love in an effort to keep it out of your life, but this does not destroy it. Even as the waves of the sea push against the barricades so does the love of God continue to push against our barricades.

As the waves of the sea are born of an infinitely higher power than we, so is God's love. We cannot destroy it any more than we can create it. This love is the same yesterday, today, tomorrow, and forevermore. It is ours to receive. It never ends.

The clearest picture of this love is not given in contemporary novels, films, plays, or poems. The clearest picture of this love is seen in an old, old story. God pours his life and love into his Son, Jesus Christ. This Son lives in the midst of us, but his life is more than we can stand. His perfection makes clear our imperfection, so there is plotting against him. Lies are told and weapons are sharpened.

Under the cloak of darkness his enemies come to arrest him. He goes with his captors unattended by his friends. There is a trial of sorts, and he is found guilty and sentenced to die by crucifixion. The crowds swell with excitement and the sky grows dark with grief. He dies sharing God's love with the soldiers who carry out the crucifixion, with the criminals who die on either side of him, and with his friends and mother who wait for lingering death to claim him.

Death comes. Darkness falls. There is a resurrection. The message rings throughout the land. He lives! He lives! He lives! God's love is victorious over death itself. The gates of hell cannot prevail against it. God's love never ends.

# 18.

*As for prophecy, it will pass away.*

Have you ever met people who got so excited about how a book was going to end that they skipped over the middle in order to read the ending and settle their anxiety? I always feel sorry for the people who yield to this temptation because they miss the middle of the book. Often it's in the middle of the book that they are shown the true nature of the characters and their lives are interwoven in such a way as to allow the author to communicate his ideas of truth to the reader. Furthermore, we may not understand the ending unless we have lived through and experienced the middle of the novel. The person who rushes to read the ending first is usually the loser.

Likewise, the people who try to skip to the end of life and get bogged down with such things as the rapture, tribulation, establishment of the kingdom, and the second coming of Christ often miss the middle. They are so concerned about how it is all going to end that they miss what's happening now. This is sad because God is doing great things in our midst today, now, this hour. Our intoxication with how God is going to complete his creation often blinds us to how God is working toward that completion at the present time.

Currently, prophecy seems to have us in a spell. It is like a magic charm in today's society. At one time, we heard about the end of time and the establishment of the kingdom only from the preacher at church. Today things have changed. Many people are talking about the end of time. Out of the movie Mecca, Hollywood, comes such a film as *The Omen*, and from the printing presses come best-selling attractions such as *The Late Great Planet Earth*. Everyone is getting into the act. Everyone wants to interpret this mysterious subject. Everyone wants to speak for God.

Naturally, we need our prophets, those who speak for God. I thank God for modern day prophets like Martin Luther King, Jr., and Senator Mark Hatfield. It is to be hoped that God will always give us men and women with such courage and insight. It is not the individual prophets who concern me but the infatuation with the whole subject of prophecy by so large a portion of the Christian population.

On the First Sunday in Lent a group of Christians attending worship services were offered an opportunity to receive a gift of one dollar, a talent dollar, to invest so it could grow. The original dollar and the profit from it were to be returned on the First Sunday in Advent. The profits were to be used to help feed hungry people around the world.

As the weeks and months went by, some of the people became excited about what was happening to the talent dollars. Some were using the original dollars to invest in making fudge while others were using it for materials for homemade crosses which were sold, and still others worked as a family and pooled their money to have sub sales. The spirit grew and the First Sunday in Advent arrived.

The people were invited to come and put their original dollars in an alms basin and the profit dollars in a harvest basket. As the people brought their money it was obvious that God had touched some of their lives. The joy of sharing was written on many faces. The people who were present in this service who had not participated in this program could not know the depth of joy experienced by those who had baked, sold, and sewed to make possible this love gift to the hungry. They could rejoice in the gift, but they knew nothing of the process and the experience of making it happen. It was the participation in the *total process* that brought deep joy, satisfaction, and meaning.

God is doing great things today. Only as we get "turned on" to what he is doing today will our infatuation with prophecy pass away, and will we believe simply with Dag Hammarskjold that "the last miracle shall be greater than the first."[7]

---

[7] *Ibid.*, p. 195.

# 19.

*As for knowledge, it will pass away.*

The film *Homo Hominis* introduces the viewer to a robot who is a great storehouse of knowledge. The robot stands much, much taller than any human being and is intricately designed. This machine man is transparent so the viewer can see all of the sophisticated network that produces these great quantities of knowledge.

The film begins when a man feeds the robot data concerning facts and figures needed for time schedules and other such intricate systems. The robot goes into its normal routine of noises and lights and out come the answers needed. Obviously, the answers are correct, and the man rewards the robot. All is well.

Next the man feeds data into the computer concerning some of the human problems of the world. There are questions about how to help the poor and how to feed the hungry. The confused robot grinds to a halt and is unable to handle the data. After some grunts and groans, the answer sheet comes out without answers. The man is frustrated, and the machine is not rewarded.

Each time hereafter when the man feeds the computer-robot data concerning facts and figures, the robot performs perfectly. It gives all of the right answers. The knowledge bank is flawless as long as it is called upon only to produce statistics. Each time the man feeds the computer moral problems concerning humans and their predicaments in this life, it is stymied. The same grunts and groans come forth but there are no solutions for humankind and their moral problems.

The man is insistent, however, and keeps trying to get the robot to answer the human needs of poverty, disease, and hunger. Finally, the computer robot is so completely exhausted by the frustration of not being able to answer the questions that it blows up. Thus comes the death of the robot. What began as a shiny knowledge bank, eager to serve and answer questions, is now a mangled mass of steel, wires, springs, and light bulbs which no longer light.

There comes a time in our life when we realize that knowledge, raw data, is not enough to answer the most important questions which face us today. The computer is limited because, in its cold calculations, it can figure the tides and tidal charts, and the flights and flight schedules, but it cannot tell us how to love one another. It cannot tell us how to limit our feverish production of arms and how to stop our hoarding and wasting of food. These are moral problems which complicate the cold statistics of life.

Many of us are born with a thirst for knowledge, and this thirst grows even stronger as we grow in our lives and see the wonders in our world waiting to be discovered. In many ways knowledge whets the appetite for more knowledge. We get "hooked" on knowledge. Some become convinced that life consists of cold and dry facts and figures. If we have knowledge we can put it all together.

For many others, however, there comes a time when we realize that knowledge is only a part of the game. The facts and figures of life begin to get tempered with sensitivity and love. Maybe this is wisdom. What is best for human beings becomes as much or more of a factor than what the statistics indicate.

In this sense, knowledge passes away. It passes into the background. This great talent which once held center stage in our life now finds itself sharing this center stage with love, emotion, and feelings. Finally, the ultimate questions in our life are not the questions which the robot computer could answer, but the ones the robot computer could not answer. These are not the questions with simple "yes" or "no" answers, but questions of morality in which we struggle to allow love to show us the way in which life is made better for more people.

Yes, that which captivated our minds in the early years now gives way to love which is a necessary ingredient as we human beings attempt to solve the problems facing us.

# 20.

*For our knowledge is imperfect and our prophecy is imperfect; but when the perfect comes, the imperfect will pass away.*

In *Fiddler on the Roof*, Tevye asks his wife, "Do you love me?" Over and over he asks her the same question. Repeatedly, his wife, Golde, tries to evade the question by reminding him that she had washed his clothes and cooked his meals and borne his children. Furthermore, she reminds him that all of these years, she has shared his bed.

None of these answers satisfies Tevye. He is not interested in the parts, the partial. He is interested in the whole, in love. "Do you love me?" Tevye knew what we all know to some extent. It is possible for a woman to share the bed and bear the child and set the table and wash the clothes and not love the one for whom she offers these services. Tevye wants the answer. "Do you love me?"

Love is wholeness or fullness, and when it comes all other gifts in this life are partial. It is like the person admiring and studying the stars at night. He is fascinated by the different constellations. He likes the lines in the sky. Then something happens. It is sunrise. The power and beauty of the sunrise cause the stars to retreat from view to the naked eye. In the light of the sun the smaller lights are put out of view. In the light of love, the smaller gifts, the partial gifts, vanish. They are still there, but they do not call attention to themselves. They are swallowed up in the larger gift, the gift of love.

When Jesus was ready to leave Peter with his ministry on our earth, he did not ask Peter if he had the courage to go out and tell the people the good news. Nor did Jesus ask him if he had sufficient knowledge to withstand the bombardment of cross examination or if he knew the strategy needed to allow the gospel message to spill out of Palestine and into the uttermost parts of the world or if he had the organizational skills to get the other disciples in line so they could be an effective team. Furthermore, he did not ask Peter about his prayer life, his ability to perform miracles, his knowledge of the future or even the peace within himself. Jesus asked Peter one simple question, "Do you love me?" (John 21:16)

When the wholeness of love comes, all the other gifts are partial. They are needed, and they are there, but in the light of the fullness of love they take their proper place. So Christ examines Peter concerning wholeness, love.

This is the same question Christ asks you and me, "Do you love me?" There may be the temptation to answer him with what we do. We serve you in your church; we talk to you in our prayers; we read your work in the Scriptures; we give a tithe of our income to charities. Despite all of these answers, the question is still before us. He is more concerned about this than about the degrees earned, the classes attended, the articles published. He is more concerned about this than about our ability to prophesy or share knowledge. He wants to know about the wholeness in our lives, love for him. Do you love me?

Answering this question in the affirmative may be a life-long process; understanding its importance is the beginning of that process. Knowing that love is the wholeness of Christ, that he wants this wholeness returned to him is where the entire process begins.

When you and I give this gift of love, all other gifts in our lives take their rightful places and perform ever greater miracles.

# 21.

When I was a child, I spoke like a child, I thought
like a child, I reasoned like a child; when I
became a man, I gave up childish ways.

### Hello, World

Hello out there, world;
It's me in here.
Can't you see me?
What? You're having trouble hearing me?

But I'm in here.
Yes, that's right.
Inside where?
Inside myself, of course.

The outside shell is very thick;
I am having trouble getting out.
Who am I? You say I don't sound like myself?
That's because you've never heard me.

This other guy? Oh, he's the shell I told you about.
You say that's me?
No, I'm in here;
He's just my protection.

Protection from what?
From you, the world.
I can't be hurt here.
You see, my shell keeps you away.

You, the world, are pain.
I'm safe in here;
I will never be laughed at.
The shell? Oh, he doesn't mind laughter.

Come to think of it,
I'm comfortable in here.
Why should I leave?
Hello, world, still listening?

What's that, world?
I thought for a minute you said something.
It was a faint voice;
It sounded human, real, I thought.
I thought it was answering me.

Maybe not.
I can't hear too well inside this shell.
Well, I feel funny, sleepy,
And it's so comfortable in here, world.

*Peter Larson, Age 14*

Dear Peter,

I have experienced with you the comfort and safety that all of us feel when we hide securely in our shells. There is embarrassment when someone laughs at us, and that's a risk we don't have to take as long as we refuse to come out of our shells. We can just stay inside our fantasy world and manipulate the other people in our lives by showing them only our shell, never our full self. The risk in shedding our shells and showing our real selves causes anxiety and a quickening pace of the heart beat. That's why some people decide to never come out of their shells. For them, life is a constant game of hide and seek.

Peter, I encourage you to consider a larger, fuller life. I hope you have experienced love. Think about the people who love you. Let their love sink deeply into you and give you the security you need to come out of your shell. Let their love remind you that the people of this world will not laugh at you, or if they do laugh, you will be strong enough to survive their laughter. Let their love penetrate more and more deeply until you begin to see in yourself something worth sharing and to see in others the ability to accept the real you and your gifts. Now let their love ease you out of your shell of fantasy and into our real world.

It will work because love is that transforming power given to each of us that helps to move us out of a world of fear and hiding and into a world of risk and sharing. It is that power which moves us from a world in which we survive in safety, into a world where we are set free to serve. Just imagine being set free to use your time, ability, and talent to love one another rather than to protect yourself in your shell.

Peter, it is not just a new birth. It's a new life! Come forth, Peter, come forth!

Love,
*Thomas C. Short, Age 41*

# 22.

*For now we see through a mirror dimly, but then face to face. Now I know in part; then I shall understand fully, even as I have been fully understood.*

I know what it is like to see through a mirror dimly. Often I rise in the morning, take a shower, and then try to shave. Naturally, I use the mirror to shave, and it is covered with steam by the humidity I have created in the small room by running hot shower water. It is irritating to try to see myself in the mirror and receive only a dull outline of what I need to see clearly. I have to keep wiping the mirror with my towel and waiting patiently for the steam to leave the room. Finally, I am able to see myself clearly and go on with the routine of my morning shave.

On an infinitely higher level, we sometimes have this same problem in our spiritual lives. Our vision of God is fogged by circumstances, hurts, anxieties, weaknesses, fears, and other hazards met in our lives. We want to see God and his mysteries and mercies clearly, but sometimes they are oblong blurs. It's like seeing through a mirror dimly. Often this frustration of not being able to see clearly gives birth to doubt, and doubt can lead to a loss of faith. These thoughts are given to us in this passage of Scripture not to bring us doubt and despair, but to remind each of us on the spiritual journey that there may be some rough spots. There are even times when what we thought we once saw clearly, we no longer see clearly. There are times when we yearn to understand more fully.

This leads us to struggle, but not to despair. In these times of spiritual crisis we "hang on," believing that someday we will see the truth "face to face" and understand fully.

In my study, I am surrounded by books of men and women of great faith. As I look at the books, I remember that these persons who experienced spiritual crises in their lives struggled and persevered and were made stronger in their faith.

One of these giants who looks at me through the books on my shelf is George Fox, the founder of the Society of Friends. In his personal journal he tells about his spiritual struggles. In his early days when he had sometimes felt more questions than answers, he talked to many counselors seeking help and advice. He was asking them to help him see more clearly the God he sought to know, love, and worship. The advice he received varied, but not much of it was helpful. One person even suggested that he start using tobacco and singing psalms. He reports that neither was a help because he did not like tobacco and wasn't in any spiritual condition to sing psalms. Then he wrote, "There was none among them all that could speak to my condition."[8]

George Fox persevered. He saw through a mirror dimly, but he pressed on with the belief that with God's help he would someday see more clearly. His vision did clear. His understanding did increase. The time came when he wrote: "Then the Lord gently led me along and let me see his love which was endless and eternal . . . this I know experimentally."

This is the promise in these words. This is the promise of God. The vision will clear. The understanding will increase. Perhaps the struggle itself is a part of the birth process to new insight and faith and knowledge.

Frederick Douglass was one of those great persons in our country who gave his strength and energy to free

---

[8] Harvey Potthoff, *A Whole Person in a Whole World* (Tennessee, 1972), p. 31.

the black people from the prisons of prejudice in which they were held captive by American whites. He bore in his body and spirit the marks of this great struggle. Often he saw through a mirror dimly, but he never ceased to persevere and to eagerly await the day when he and others could see truth being done. He wrote:

> If there is no struggle, there is no progress. Those who profess to favor freedom, and yet deprecate agitation are men who want crops without plowing up the ground. They want the ocean without the awful roar of its many waters.[9]

---

[9] Robert Goldston, *The Negro Revolution*, (New York, 1968), p. 199.

# 23.

*So faith . . . abides.*

The car went speeding by with a bright yellow and black bumper sticker staring at me. It read: "I found it!" This particular bumper sticker refers to faith. It is a proclamation: "I found it!" Not, by God's grace, I believe, but "I found it!" Faith is often seen as the end result of our own efforts, as the fabric we weave with our own human hands and imaginations.

The temptation to make faith the work of our own hands is alive and well. The tempter suggests to us that by reading the Scriptures regularly, saying our prayers daily, worshiping with our fellow Christians weekly, and giving at least ten percent of our income to the church, we will have faith and have it abundantly. In these situations, faith becomes a degree to be earned. It is seen as the end result of all our arduous labors and works.

Perhaps we lean in this direction because we live in an earning-centered society. We are trained to believe that whatever is good and noble has to be earned. We don't get something for nothing. Consequently, in our earliest years some of us are taught that we are to earn our dessert by eating all of our dinner. The process continues in school when the child is taught to earn good grades. After school, the motive is money and status. If we are going to have money, status, and position, we are going to have to work for it. It will not come easily. Obviously, we are a part of an earning-centered culture. Somehow most of us are taught well that you don't get something for nothing.

In matters of faith, we are tempted to carry over the same logic. If we are going to get it, we are going to have to earn it. The tendency is to set up structural "do's" and "don't's" so we can convince ourselves and others that we have earned the precious gift of faith. It is all so natural.

It is also catastrophic. There are occasions in life when our human resources wear thin and we are filled with self-doubt. At such times the things which we have created have a tendency to be threatened. If faith is a fabric we have woven with our own ingenuity, it becomes suspect in such times of self-doubt. Conversely, if we come to our faith by God's grace (love) then he is one whom we can trust even in our hour of self-doubt. He becomes an island in our troubled sea.

The English word "gospel" comes from a combination of "God" and "spell" (story). The gospel is God's story. It is the story of what God has done and is doing in the lives of his people. Throughout this story of God's actions in our lives, God is the key. He is the one who begins the action, the initiator. Due to his action the world was brought into being, Abraham left his homeland to go and seek another place, the captive children of Israel were set free from the bondage of the Egyptians, Mary conceived and brought forth her first born child and wrapped him in swaddling clothes and laid him in a manger, and the Holy Spirit broke into the lives of the disciples at Pentecost. In all of these cases from his story, God acts and human beings react. Human beings receive the initiative of God and respond to it.

Suddenly, the whole order is reversed. Faith is not something which we earn. Faith is the gift of God himself. Through his story, his Son and his Holy Spirit, he comes to us and acts in us so that as many as are willing to receive his gift of love are encouraged to trust him, to have faith in him.

Faith is growing to trust God's actions, his love. It is not growing to trust in our schemes and systems. This is why the Scriptures indicate that faith will last forever. Faith built upon our own works, our own foundations, is like the man who built his house upon the sand. The storms came and the sands eroded, and the foundations gave way until the house collapsed. Faith built upon God's love and actions is like the man who built his house upon the rock. The storms came and beat upon that house and it did not fall. This house lasts forever.

# 24.

*The greatest of these is love.*

In Dostoevski's *Brothers Karamazov*, the dying monk, Father Zessima, says to Alyesha:

*And let not men's sin dishearten thee: love a man even in his sin, for that love is a likeness of the divine love, and is the summit of love on earth. Love all God's creation, both the whole and every grain of sand. Love every leaf, every ray of light. Love the animals, love the plants, love each separate thing. If thou love each thing thou wilt perceive the mystery of love in all; and when once thou perceive this, thou wilt thenceforward grow every day to a fuller understanding of it: until thou come at last to love the whole world with a love that will then be all-embracing and universal.*

This love continues to work throughout the Christian church opening hearts and minds formerly closed to one another. Worship, marriage, and fellowship in the church have been enriched because of this love. Consequently, it has encouraged countless thousands to be able to receive the gifts of faith and hope.

The mystery of love grows in a human life and becomes more and more of a powerful force. This is one of the reasons it is the greatest gift. We have seen the words and thoughts of Dostoevski leap to life in the lives of some of our brothers and sisters. One who comes quickly to my mind is Pope John XXIII. It was the day after Christmas when he stood among the thousand prisoners in loose-fitting, drab, convict-striped uniforms who had assembled to greet him when he visited their prison in Rome. These same prisoners who surrounded him in a great wall of humanity were the ones who had made an exquisite creche that had touched the Pope as he entered the gloomy rotunda. He called them "sons and brothers" and shared with them out of his own experience and life. The prisoners were touched by his love and felt his dynamic power.

One of the older prisoners who had a long police record asked the Pope if his message of hope were also for him. The prisoner made his confession; the Pope bent over the kneeling man, wiped away his tears, raised him to his feet, gave him a big bear hug and said, "I have put my heart near your heart."

Finally, the Pope came to the cell block for the incorrigibles who were confined and under heavy security. In a strong voice John said, "Open the gates. Do not bar them from me. They are all children of our Lord." With that the gates were lowered and the Pope's love was shared with these persons also.

Isn't this the promise to which Dostoevski points in the passage above? To receive the gift of love and to share the gift of love is the only way to "come at last to love the whole world with a love that will then be all-embracing and universal." To receive the gift and to share the gift is to come at last to love the imprisoned incorrigibles of the prison as well as the kings and queens of this world.

God gives us this gift in Jesus Christ and encourages us to share this gift in our daily living. It is the greatest gift not only because it is the gift which grows by usage, but because it is the stability of other good gifts like hope, faith, patience, kindness, humility, and wisdom.

It is the greatest gift not only because it opens prison gates but also because it opens human hearts so that people can live more freely and creatively.

It is the greatest gift not only because it takes us up to the very footstool of our Creator but also because it takes us down to the depth of our own being, our own humanity.

It is the greatest gift not only because it helps us to see ourselves as beautiful and unique in the mind of our Creator, but it also enables us to see other beautiful and unique people as our brothers and sisters.

It is the greatest gift not only because it is the link between ourselves and our Lord but also because it is the link between ourselves and every living creature.

Thanks be to God who gives us the gift of love and those good witnesses who have received and shared it in such a way as to make it more inviting and available to each of us.